A Pet Hen

Written by Fran Quinn
Illustrated by Jason Edwards

Phonics Skill

Short e

Peg	met	Ned	pet
Hen	pen	bed	get
fed	let		

Peg met Ned.
Peg got a pet from Ned.
Here is Hen.

Did Hen have a pen?
Hen did not.

Peg got Hen a pen.
Go in, Hen.

Did Hen have a bed?
Hen did not.

Peg got Hen a bed.
Get in, Hen.

Peg fed Hen.

Peg got in bed.
Let Peg nap, Hen.